THE GOSPEL TO THE CHOCTAW

by Claude Gilbert

with a biography of

REV. ROBERT BELL

by Richard Beard

Memphis, Tennessee
Cumberland Presbyterian Church
2015

©**2015** by the Cumberland Presbyterian Church. Prepared by members of the Discipleship Ministry and Missions Ministry Teams of the Ministry Council of the Cumberland Presbyterian Church with additional material provided by the Historical Foundation of the Cumberland Presbyterian Church and the Cumberland Presbyterian Church in America. Maps from the Wikimedia Commons.

All Rights Reserved. No part of this book may be reproduced or transmitted in any form or by any means, electronic or mechanical, including photocopying, recording, or by any information storage or retrieval system, without permission in writing from the publisher. For information address Discipleship Ministry Team, Cumberland Presbyterian Center, 8207 Traditional Place, Cordova (Memphis), Tennessee, 38016-7414.

The primary portion of this book was originally published by the Board of Missions of the Cumberland Presbyterian Church in 1968. Although many circumstances remain the same, the period in which the original manuscript was prepared should be kept in mind when reading this volume. Except for minor corrections, no changes have been made to the original text.

Funded, in part, by your contributions to Our United Outreach.

First printing in this format, July 2015.
Second printing, May 2018.

ISBN-13: 978-0692486313
ISBN-10: 0692486313

OUR UNITED OUTREACH
Made Possible In Part By Your Tithe To Our United Outreach

CONTENTS

Preface by Rev. T. J. Malinoski. vii

Maps. ix

The Gospel to the Choctaw by Claude Gilbert. 1
    Removal of the Choctaws. 7
    The Remaining Tribes. 12
    Choctaw Government in Oklahoma. 18
    Education Among the Choctaws. 21
    The Civil War in the Choctaw Nation. 26
    Reconstruction. 30
    The Cumberland Presbyterian Church in Oklahoma
    36
    Choctaw Presbytery Today. 43
    Future Needs of the Choctaw. 48
    Acknowledgments. 53

Rev. Robert Bell by Richard Beard. 55

What life have you if you have not life together?
There is no life that is not in community,
And no community not lived in praise of God?

T.S. Eliot, Choruses from *The Rock*[1]

PREFACE

Claude Gilbert's *The Gospel to the Choctaw* is a brief narrative about the intrinsic connection between the life of the Cumberland Presbyterian Church and the Choctaw Nation. A fledgling denomination, whose existence was still uncertain and could easily have disappeared into the wilderness of the eastern frontiers of a young nation, found itself among the Choctaw peoples.

This book is also a recounting of the evolution of Cumberland Presbyterian mission work. The idea of entering a "foreign field" to share the gospel of Jesus Christ has transitioned and transformed to creating community. T.S. Eliot poses the question succinctly, "What life have you if you have not life together?" Living together in community requires patience and understanding. Human history has shown how varied and complex, frightening and fragile life is. Being a community in praise of God magnifies how awesome and delightful, and more beautiful and strong life is when we are together.

The Cumberland Presbyterian narrative has been bestowed the gift of community from the Choctaws during its two hundred plus years filled with adversity, dignity and

---

[1]F.B. Pinion, *A T.S. Eliot Companion* (Macmillian Press Limited: London, 1986), 209.

confidence in the future. This gift of community has helped shape the story of how we became the Cumberland Presbyterian people that we are and why we think and feel the way we do.

In essence, the **Gospel to the Choctaw** is just one narrative. It is the retelling of two peoples whose enthusiasm for Christ become one, combining tragedy with perseverance, offenses with friendship and injustice with love. The Choctaw Cumberland Presbyterians have exemplified Eliot's words, "There is no life that is not in community. And no community not lived in praise of God."

Rev. T. J. Malinoski
Evangelism and New Church Development
Missions Ministry Team, CPC
May 2018

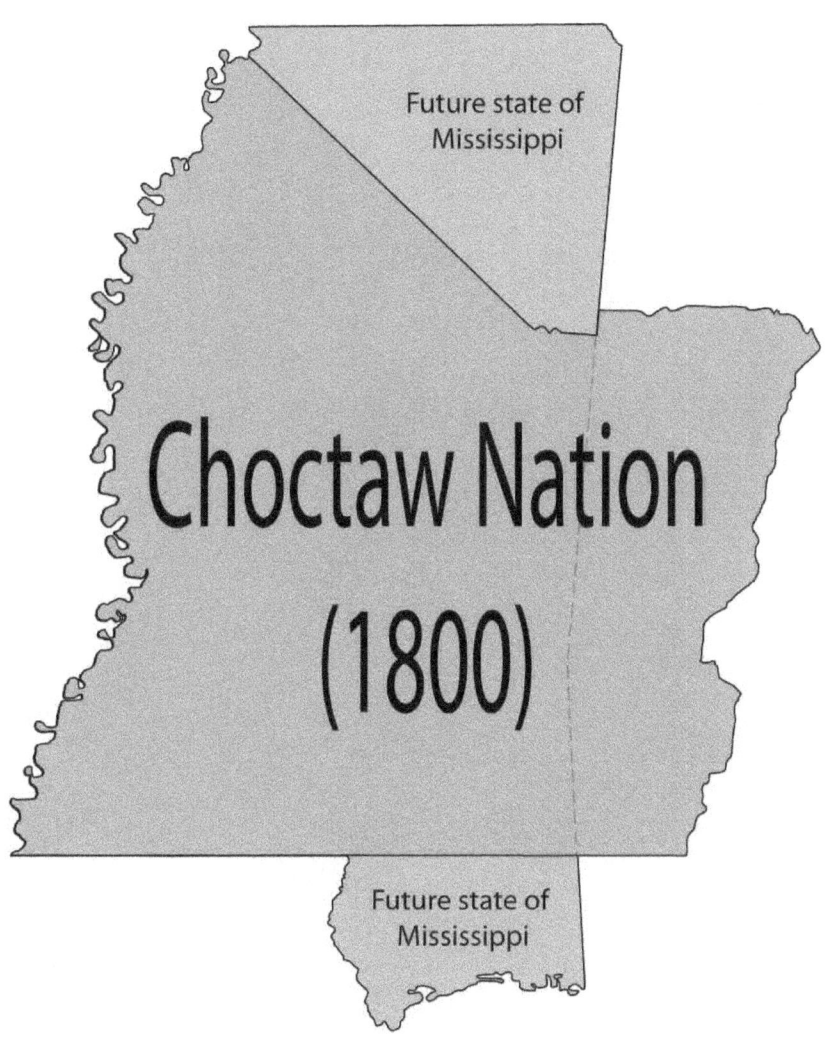

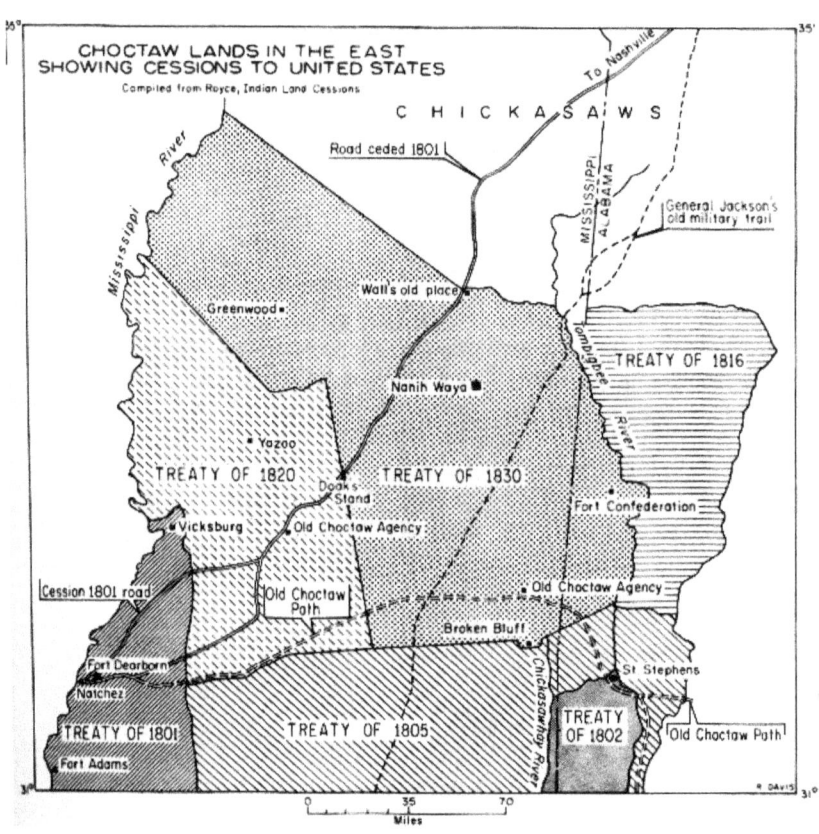

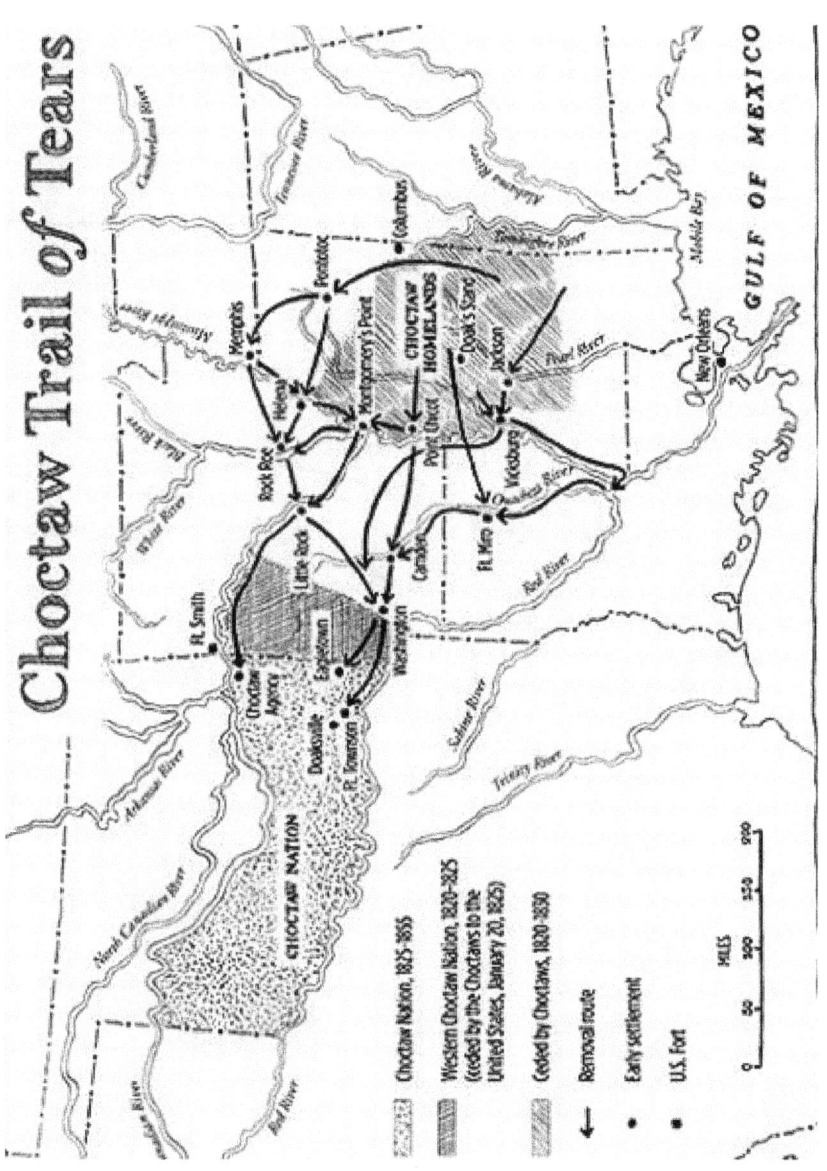

Choctaw Nation in Oklahoma

The Gospel to the Choctaw

By Claude Gilbert

On a brisk October morning in the year 1818, three horsemen forded the Tombigbee River in present-day Mississippi, and rode slowly to the center of a large clearing in which were located about twenty-five log cabins and earth-covered shelters. At a signal from the guide, the three men halted and the guide rode another fifty yards, dismounting before a group of thirty armed Indian men. The half breed guide spoke in the language of his mother but his flailing arms testified to the French blood of his father as he punctuated each statement with broad gestures.

Presently he followed the Choctaw men to a large cabin in the center of the clearing into which the entire group disappeared. The two white men waited, a bit nervously, as they sat on their mounts and surveyed these unfamiliar surroundings. What had appeared to be a small clearing where the huts were located was in reality only a part of a large clearing two miles in circumference, broken by wind-rows of timber.

The village was located on the highest level of the plain. In the distance could be seen large cultivated fields.

The cabins were much like other log structures common on the frontier, except somewhat smaller, most consisting of only one room. Although chimneys were not in evidence, smoke could be seen rising from the center of several cabins through smoke holes. Several cooking fires could be seen outside the cabins.

From where the two men sat they could see ten strange scaffolds, about twelve feet high, and located twenty to thirty feet from the cabins. These scaffolds were made of poles, the top being floored solid, and on each scaffold was a hide-wrapped object that roughly outlined the form of a human body. These were the funeral scaffolds of the Choctaw.

The village seemed to be deserted except for an occasional glimpse of a child or a woman peering from a doorway or from behind a tree.

About half an hour elapsed before the guide reappeared, followed by a large group of men. The two white men were much relieved to note that no weapons were in evidence. The whole company approached the two mounted men, their dark eyes reflecting warmth and friendship. Broad smiles covered their faces as the guide threw up his left hand, gesturing toward the visitors as he announced in a loud voice, "*ltibapishi* Samuel King and William Moore." The gospel had come to the Choctaw.

King and Moore spent almost six months in the Choctaw nation, traveling from village to village, speaking to the *Mingos*, (the head men) , and the warriors, preaching the gospel of Jesus Christ, and mapping the territory.

These two ministers had been commissioned by Elk Presbytery of the Cumberland Presbyterian Church in the fall of 1818 to travel through the Indian country to ascertain the need and the prospeot of future work among them. Aside from being the first Protestant ministers to preach the gospel effectively ito the Choctaw, King and Moore were the first *foreign* missionaries of the infant Cumberland Presbyterian Church. The Choctaw nation was considered "foreign" since it had its own government and held treaty rights with the United States. Their visit marked the beginning of a ministry and friendship between the Cumberland Presbyterian Church and the Choctaw people that continues to this day.

Upon their return the missionaries reported to Elk Presbytery and to the newly organized Mission Society. The prospect for fruitful work among the Indians seemed promising. The need was great and the desire for the gospel on the parit of the Choctaw seemed sincere. The two men strongly recommended that a school be established among the Indians for the purpose of establishing the Christian faith in the life of the people and to teach the children the ways of civilization and better methods of farming.

The report was well received and no time was lost in planning the new venture. First, a man had to be found who had a burning desire to fulfill the Lord's command to "Go into all the world and preach the gospel." The person for the mission would have to be a man who was void of all self-interest, or concern for self-comfort or gain.

Such a man was found in the Rev. Robert Bell, one of the "young men" of the revival party who had already risked all through his conviction of what was good and right for the church. That same year, 1819, Mr. Bell and his family departed for the Indian country. He intiated a work that consumed much of his remaining years, first in the ancient land of the Choctaw and Chickasaw and later in the new land of Oklahoma.

Reversals and hardships which would have discouraged lesser men seemed only to spur Bell on to greater efforts. Original plans for a school among the Choctaw were almost immediately thwarted. The success of King and Moore in their stay among the Choctaw, and the desire of the Choctaw people to accept missionaries and schools within their territory, had opened a flood gate to Christian churches and missionary groups anxious to share the Christian gospel. Among these was the American Board of Commissioners for Foreign Missions which enjoyed federal support and the financial backing of ithe Presbyterian and Congregationalist churches.

Bell's school could not survive without the federal grant provided for such ventures. This grant went to the American Board. Another factor was the signing of the Treaty of Doak's Stand, which provided for the eventual removal of the Choctaws to the West. Bell established his school in the Chickasaw nation.

For twelve years Bell labored among the Chickasaw, assisted by his family and a rapid turnover of assistants. Due to the extreme hardships encountered, help was difficult to get and harder to keep. Often the Bell children had to function as instructors. To add to the difficulty, Bell had to make frequent trips to the "States" to secure funds and food for the thirty-five to forty children in his charge.

Even in this early day there was opposition to missions. Bell met this opposition head-on. When objections or dissatisfaction were voiced to the project, he invited the complainant to visit the field. When the dissenter viewed firsthand the extreme spiritual poverty of the people, and othe lasting effect of the work, objection to the project turned to enthusiasm. To quote Mr. Bell, "Oh that all the people who oppose the mission would make us a visit."

During the twelve years the mission existed in the Chickasaw nation, Bell received an average of $300 per year from the United States government, plus the support given by the church. The greatest amount received from all sources in one year was $1494; the least amount received was $369.

With ithis amount the mission was supported, materials necessary for study and farming were purchased, and Mr. Bell's family and the student body were fed and clothed.

Due to the ratification of the treaty of removal between the government and the Chickasaw people, all government and church aid was cut off in 1830. Inasmuch as ·the actual removal did not take place for about four years, Bell continued the school for two years longer. The expense of the school was met with funds from Mr. Bell's own estate.

Removal of the Choctaws

In 1820, at Doak's Stand, the chiefs of .the Choctaw nation finally yielded to their covetous white neighbors and ithe undisguised threats of the federal government, and signed .the Treaty of Removal .that is still known as the Treaty of Doak's Stand. The treaty provided for the voluntary removal of all Choctaw people from east of the Mississippi to new lands in the Indian Territory. The relinquishing of all lands then held by the tribe and a planned schedule for removal was agreed to.

In exchange the Choctaws were to receive a tract of land in the West, bordered on the east by the territory of Arkansas, on the south by the Red River, on the north by the Arkansas and Canadian rivers, and on the west by the one hundredth meridian. These boundaries included approximately one-half of what is now the state of Oklahoma.

Each Choctaw man was to receive a new gun, a lead mold, and powder and lead to last one year. The federal government guaranteed protection from all enemies and a guarantee that no white man would ever be allowed in the new nation. Terms of the treaty stated that this territory would never be incorporated into a state. The land would belong to the Choctaw, "As long as the grass grows and the rivers flow."

Pushmataha

At the time of the signing of the Treaty of Doak's Stand the principal chief of the Choctaws was the legendary Apushmataha, the greatest of Choctaw warriors and statesmen. Though dissatisfied with the terms of the treaty, he signed. Then he left immediately for Washing- ton where he spent the few remaining years of his life securing better terms for his people. As a result of his labors a new treaty, known as the Treaty of Dancing Rabbit Creek, was signed at a place bearing that name on September 28, 1830. It was basically the same as the Treaty of Doak's Stand with a few important changes.

The new treaty provided that fifty four sections of the best land in Mississippi be sold at auction and the money be used for ithe future education of the Choctaw children. Another important provision was for the payment of annuities to the people following their arrival in the new land. These payments were ito be at government expense for the first year, then were to continue from tribal funds held in trust by the government. The treaty also provided for additional personal items to be provided for the Indian households, such as spinning wheels, plows, and harness.

The most significant provision allowed any Choctaw who so wished to remain in Mississippi, on allotted lands, under the laws of the state. Some 4,500 people chose to leave the Choctaw nation and become citizens of that state. Today approximately 2,500 Choctaws remain in Mississippi. They are known as Mississippi Choctaws.

The Choctaws were the first of the Five Civilized Tribes to be removed from their lands in the East to Oklahoma. The journey that began in the fall of 1832 is remembered in history as the Trail of Tears.

The government bore the expense and the responsibility for getting the people to their new homes. The wisdom of Apushmataha (now spelled Pushmataha) had failed to foresee the dangers of this arrangement. In the typical manner of the government of that day little planning went into the project. The chief concern was for the quickest and least expensive method of accomplishing the task. Civilian contractors were hired to furnish the transportation and food for the journey. One wagon for every eighty people was provid ed for hauling baggage. Payment was made at $20 per head. The army went along to insure that there would be no stragglers and no changing of minds once the journey began.

The trip was made as far as possible by steamboat. From a point near Camden, Arkansas, the Indians disembarked and the people walked in subfreezmg weather. Only the sick and the very young found room to ride on the baggage wagons. The greed of the contractors had reduced the people to a state of near starvation. Exposure and an epidemic of cholera added to their suffering. It is estimated that one out of four who started the journe y failed to arrive in the new land. About four thousand died along the way—mainly children and the elderly.

Upon arrival the people set themselves at the task of building homes and clearing land. By the spnng of 1833 the first arrivals had planted crops. Then another disaster struck. The worst flood in the history of the territory swept the new

Choctaw nation. Crops, homes, and hvestock were washed away. The people continued to starve.

The Remaining Tribes

Despite the terrible sufferings of the Choctaw, time proved them to be the lucky ones. Their kinsmen, the Cherokee, Creeks, Chickasaws, and Seminoles, did not fare so well.

Divisions within the Cherokee tribe delayed their removal. Finally the Cherokee National Council declared their treaty invalid, saying that by Cherokee law no chief or group of chiefs had the authority to sell tribal lands. So violent was this division that the principal chief who had signed the treaty feared for his life. This division did not end with the removal, but continues even today.

The treaty party leaders were Major Ridge, Iohn Ridge, Elias Boudinot, and Stand Watie. In June of 1839, several years after removal Major Ridge, John Ridge, and Elias Boudinot were assassinated and Stand Watie was marked for death. He faced down the assassins, offered a $10,000 reward for the names of their leaders, then turned and walked away from them. He later became a brigadier general in the Confederate cavalry.

Following the refusal of the Cherokee to give up their land, the citizens of the state of Georgia took matters into their own hands. The persecution that followed is unequaled in the history of the United States. Th Georgia state government passed laws abolishing the Cherokee constitution, making the people subject to state law. Another law was passed that made the testimony of a Cherokee inadmissible in the courts. Immediately suits were filed against individual Cherokees claiming theft of livestock and other property. White citizens laid claim to houses, mills, and other property of the Indians.

Since Cherokee testimony was inadmissible in the courts, the white citizens won their cases and stripped the people of all property of value with the exception of tribal lands. The state also passed laws making it illegal for non-Indians to travel in Indian country, without a special permit. These permits were readily available to prospectors who desired to mine in the newly discovered gold fields located in the Cherokee nation.

No minister or missionary was given a permit. Officials explained this by saying the missionaries were encouraging the Indians to stay on their lands. In one instance twelve missionaries refused to leave. They were arrested and threatened with prison unless they agreed to leave. Nine of the men yielded and departed. Three refused, were tried, convicted, and sentenced to prison. These three men appealed to the United States Supreme Court. That high tribunal overturned the conviction and ordered the release of the missionaries. Then followed one of the greatest injustices ever to come from the national Capitol. President Jackson, under whose administration more atrocities against the

Indians were committed than any other, refused to order the carrying out of the court's instructions. The missionaries remained imprisoned.

Finally the army was ordered to remove the Cherokees by force. No time was lost in carrying out the order. A stockade was readied. The army went into the Indian country in squads. Like herding cattle, the people were driven into the stockade. There was no delay and no exception. The old, the sick, and the able-bodied were driven in. No time was allowed for the collection of personal property. Doors were broken down and families were surprised at meal time or in their beds and were driven to the stockade. Looters followed the army, and in many cases homes were in flames and possessions were divided among the thieves before the family was out of sight.

The Cherokees suffered more on the trail than did the Choctaws. Their route was more northerly, and they walked most of the way.

The Chickasaws and Creeks suffered much the same as did the Choctaws and Cherokees. The loss of life was not so great since their removal took place during the summer and fall. The Choctaws, being close relatives to the Chickasaws, did much to relieve, their suffering upon their arrival in the new land.

The Seminoles resisted removal more strenuously than did any of the other tribes. Their long and gallant fight for their country would require volumes to tell. The removal of the Seminoles was the most expensive venture the government ever undertook in its dealings with the Indians of the Southeast. Efforts toward removal began in 1832. By 1842 the government succeeded in removing three thousand Seminoles to Oklahoma. Few of these came peacefully. The cost of keeping the army in the field during this time is reported at $20,000,000. More than 1,500 soldiers were killed in the fighting, with countless others maimed for life. For each Seminole removed to Indian territory, the government cost was $6,500. For every two Seminoles removed to the West the army paid with the life of one soldier.

The Seminole removal brought to a close one of the blackest periods m American history. The Trail of Tears of the Five Civilized Tribes a people ruthlessly uprooted to make room for the white settlers ranks with the tragedies of the ages.

Angry protest by tribal leaders and charges of profiteering and fraud cause the federal government to investigate the removal contractors. Major Ethan Allen Hitchcock was ordered to Indian Territory to look into the complaints. Concerning his appointment John R. Swanton has said, "Since the national administration was willing to look the other way while this criminal operation (the removal) was in progress, it made a curious blunder in permitting the injunction into such a situation of an investigator as little disposed to whitewash iniquity as was Ethan Allen Hitchcock."

Major Hitchcock arrived in Indian territory during November 1841. He wasted little time in questioning officials and contractors. He went directly to the various towns of the Five Civilized Tribes and talked to the Indians themselves. In one instance he found that a contractor who had settled on the border, "came here so poor that a man with $400 claim against him was glad to settle for $100. Now he owns a considerable number of Negroes and has offered $17,500 for a plantation." His exhaustive investigation yielded evidence that "bribery, perjury, and forgery, short weights, issues of spoiled meat and grain, and every conceivable subterfuge was employed by designing white men on the Indians."

Hitchcock took his findings to Washington where he prepared a report with one hundred exhibits attached, and filed this heavy document with the Secretary of War. Committees of Congress tried vainly to have it submitted to them so that appropriate action could be taken but it was stated that "too many friends of the administration were involved to permit the report to become public. It disappeared from the files and no trace of it is to be found." The fact that the report and its findings were not made public and the disappearance of the report from official files proves the honesty of the report and the dishonesty of the national administration of the period.

Ethan Allen Hitchcock

Choctaw Government in Oklahoma

Oklahoma politics did not begin in 1907 with statehood. Oklahoma politics was born out of the agony of removal and the painful readjustment to a new land. The Choctaw were the first of the Five Civilized Tribes to organize constitutional government in Oklahoma. The people had adopted a written code of laws prior to the removal by which private action through the primitive personal revenge code was replaced by public law which made crimes against persons and property offenses against the nation. In 1826 the Choctaw adopted a written constitution which contained a curious blending of ancient tribal practice and new thought.

From earliest times the Choctaw government had consisted of a council composed of warriors, leading men, and three principal chiefs. The office of chief had usually been hereditary, descent being traced through the females of the line under the clan system. Thus a son could not succeed his father as chief. Only the chief's sister's son was eligible. At the time of removal, the district chiefs were Nitakechi (Apushmataha's nephew) for the southeast or southern district, Greenwood LeFlore in the western district, and Moshultaubbee in the northeast district.

Just before departing in 1832 the three chiefs met, studied a map of the western country and assigned a district to each. LeFlore's constituency was to settle in the country east of the Kiamichi; Moshulatubbee's district was established on the Arkansas and Canadian; and Nitakechi selected a district west of the Kiamichi.

The constitutional history of the Choctaws in Oklahoma began in 1834 when tribal leaders gathered at a trading post on the Kiamichi, halfway between the Red and the Arkansas, to hold their first general council in the West. Their work resulted in the first constitution written in Oklahoma. The system of three principal chiefs continued. The settled portion of the Choctaw nation was divided into the familiar three districts, each serving as oa constituency for a particular chief executive. The chiefs were elected and served four-year terms. No chief could serve more than two terms.

Oklahoma's first constitution also contained a bill of rights, established an elective National Council of twenty-seven members (nine from each district) chosen annually, and a national court system (elective judgeships). For defense, a militia was provided for in a general who was elected by the people and thirty-two captains in each district, each responsible for mustering his quota of troops. Eighteen light-horsemen (six in each district) were to enforce the laws of the National Council.

The bill of rights of the Choctaw constitution included jury trial, and defined eligible voters as all male citizens, twenty-one years of age or over. The Choctaw National Council met annually for about two weeks, elected a speaker, and conducted the legislative business of the nation. The three chiefs occupied the seats of honor in the Council house, which was a hewn log structure situated at a settlement designated as the Choctaw National Capital and called "Nanih Wayah" (leaning hill). It was located near the town of Tuskahoma.

     Each of the chiefs reported on conditions in his district and made recommendations for legislation. The constitution vested the chiefs with veto power (two of the three were necessary to negate), and the Council could override an executive veto with a two-thirds vote.

Education Among the Choctaws

One of the major concerns of the Choctaw National Council was providing for the education of the children. Schools were established throughout the Choctaw Nation. Some of the schools were under the direction of various missionary boards. However in every case the National Council set the requirements and supervised the schools.

The curriculum of Choctaw schools was diversified. The students were taught a variety of vocational subjects in addition to the traditional subjects of spelling, biology, history, astronomy, Latin, Greek, English, arithmetic, philosophy, and in the mission schools Bible studies. The boys were trained in animal husbandry, agriculture, the mechanical arts, and carpentry, while the girls were instructed in child care, cooking, and other domestic arts. The school system in the Choctaw nation pioneered in the area of special education. This system included schools for orphans and children from broken homes, and instruction for the deaf, blind, and mentally ill.

By 1838 the American Board mission schools in the Choctaw nation numbered ten. In addition to maintaining regular school and mission programs through the week, American Board workers attracted parents of the students with a pioneer effort in adult education through Sabbath schools and weekend camps. These weekly gatherings which offered elementary instruction in reading, writing, spelling, and arithmetic helped to wipe out illiteracy in the Choctaw nation. This break-through in Choctaw learning resulted from the efforts of American Board teacher, the Rev. Cyrus Byington, who, after years of study, was able to reduce the Choctaw spoken language to written forms by using the English alphabet. He published the first Choctaw grammar in 1834. The National Council gave much support to these mission schools. In 1842 alone the Council appropriated $26,000, a substantial sum for the times, for their support.

Cyrus Byington

As the Choctaw advanced in learning, the neighborhood schools were found to supply only the foundation for an education. The demand for advanced learning was met during the 1840s by the construction of academies at key locations in the nation. In 1841 the Choctaw National Council enacted legislation providing for the erection of an institution for advanced study for boys, near Doaksville. The school was named Spencer Academy in honor of Secretary of War, John C. Spencer, who had given sustained encouragement and support to the Choctaws in their drive for the best possible education.

Spencer Academy opened in 1844 under the leadership of Edward McKinney and functioned for nearly two years as an institution of the Choctaw nation. The new academy failed to develop as rapidly as expected, so the National Council placed it under the direction of the Presbyterian Board of Foreign Missions, supported by tribal funds, with James B. Ramsey as superintendent. The development and operation of the academy system in the Choctaw nation involved religious groups other than the Presbyterians and Congregationalists. Methodists, Baptists, and Cumberland Presbyterians played an important role in the founding and operation of these institutions.

The largest and most successful was Armstrong Academy, located in the southwestern portion of the nation. Armstrong Academy was opened in 1844, under the direction of the Baptist Home Mission Board. Dissatisfaction with its operation led the Council, in 1858, to assign this school to the Cumberland Presbyterian Church Board.

Armstrong Academy

The outstanding graduates of these academies were granted scholarships by the National Council, enabling them to complete their education in colleges and universities in the East. Before the Civil War, the Choctaw nation counted graduates of Dartmouth, Union, and Yale among its citizens.

The neighboring Chickasaw nation followed the lead of their Choctaw kinsmen in establishing their educational system. During the 1850s several academies were constructed with tribal funds. One of these was Burney Institute.

In 1817, the Rev. Robert Bell had visited the Chickasaws. In 1820 he had established the first school among them, some ten years before other Christian mission societies reached the Chickasaws. It is to the honor of this great man, and a testimony to his effectiveness that the Chickasaw National Council requested the Cumberland Presbyterian Board to send Mr. Bell to superintend this new academy. It is also to the honor of Mr. Bell that he was the only white minister to remain at his post throughout the trying and dangerous period of the Civil War. For the greater part of the conflict the Rev. Mr. Bell was unaided and out of contact with his church.

In the early years following removal, the greatest contribution made by the Cumberland Presbyterian Church was in the leadership given the Choctaw and Chickasaw people in the area of education, especially in the academy system.

During the years between 1832 and 1860 there seems to have been no shortage of missionaries willing to serve among the Indians. Every major denomination and missionary society seemed anxious to help. The real need seems to have been for teachers. The Choctaw, taking advantage of this situation, required each church or society to send one teacher for every minister who worked among them.

It is a credit to the memory of Samuel King and William Moore that even in this time of plenty the Choctaw people repeatedly petitioned the Cumberland Presbyterian Board to send ministers to them. Some of the letters were addressed directly to King many years after his death. It appears that the "one minister-one teacher" ratio was not required in the case of Cumberland Presbyterian ministers.

The Civil War in the Choctaw Nation

The years between the removal of the Choctaws to Oklahoma and the beginning of the Civil War can be described as the "golden years" of the Choctaw. The Christian religion had found an abiding place in their lives. The entire nation was quickly becoming educated and prosperous. Many of the prominent families owned large plantations, large numbers of slaves, and great wealth. There was a ready market for their goods in New Orleans. The waterways provided transportation for these products. A strong constitutional government provided protection and continued prosperity.

Then the dark cloud of disaster once again began to appear. Again the greedy eyes of the land hungry white man looked longingly in the direction of the Indian country. The strong railroad lobby in Washington continued to press for right-of-way across the Indian Territory, demanding the customary 3,600,000 acres of land as a subsidy for building its line. The United States government was searching for a home for other uprooted Indian tribes who had fallen to the constant pressure of the western movement. The Indian lands in Oklahoma seemed to be the answer to all these problems. The one thing that stood in the way were the unconditional and binding treaties with the Five Civilized Tribes. The Civil War provided the excuse for breaking them.

The unbelievable suffering of the Indian tribes during the Civil War cannot be told in this brief narrative. The death, famine, exposure, and injustice that shook the nation from one end to the other can be charged to both the federal government and the Confederacy.

At the beginning of hostilities the Choctaw sided with the South. Due to their geographical location, neutrality was impossible. To cast their lot with the South was to be expected. The Choctaw remembered the past and continuing injustices of the federal government too well. Then too, the Choctaw held many slaves, and much of the economy depended on the continuation of this system.

Though the Choctaw proved a capable and trustworthy ally, the Confederacy failed almost immediately to keep faith with them. In the treaty with the South it was agreed that the Choctaw soldier would not have to fight outside his own territory. The Confederacy promised to supply the necessary food and supplies to sustain the people. In addition, Confederate troops were promised for border protection. All these conditions were violated the first year of the war. Choctaw troops were ordered into several battles in Arkansas. Provisions were inadequate, causing great suffering since all the Choctaw nation's money was held in trust by the federal government. The Union cavalry raided at will from its bases in Kansas.

General Stand Watie

In the last year of the war the Choctaw troops were placed under the command of General Stand Watie, a Cherokee, the only Indian to attain that rank in either the

Union or Confederate armies. General Watie's greatest victory of the war occurred in September 1864, at Cabin Creek crossing. A supply train of three hundred wagons under heavy military guard, en route from Fort Scott to Port Gibson, was captured by Watie and his cavalry. He drove the prize into Confederate territory where the store of food, medical supplies, clothing, and blankets was distributed among the Indian refugee camps.

In another unusual feat, General Watie's scouts discovered a slow moving steamship on the Arkansas River, loaded with Union supplies. At Pleasant Bluff, just below the mouth of the Canadian, the colorful Watie swept from ambush and captured the ship with a cavalry charge. Great quantities of food, blankets, and medical supplies fell to the Confederates by this feat. General Watie's troops were among the last of the Confederate forces to surrender.

Reconstruction

Representatives of the five tribes were directed to meet at Ft. Smith to discuss terms for resuming relations with the United States. The council took place on September 8, 1865 and lasted thirteen days. The United States commissioners opened the council with the statement ,that the Five Civilized Tribes, having violated their treaties with the United States, had thereby forfeited all rights under these treaties, and that consequently each tribe must consider itself at the mercy of the United States.

The conditions for resuming relations with the United States were set forth: (1) each tribe must enter into a treaty for permanent peace and amity among themselves, and with the United States; (2) slavery must be abolished and steps taken to incorporate the freedmen into the tribes as citizens, with rights guaranteed; (3) each tribe must agree to surrender a portion of its lands to the United States for colonizing tribes from Kansas and elsewhere; (4) they must agree to the policy of uniting all the tribes in the Indian Territory into a single, consolidated government.

The tribal delegations were shocked at the extreme demands of the federal government and deliberately delayed the proceedings. Finally the government commission decided they would be unable to close the reconstruction treaties at Ft. Smith and recessed the council, calling for a resumption of negotiations at Washington the following year. The reasoning of the commissioners was that, removed from the influence and pressures of their fellow tribesmen, the representatives would be easier to deal with.

During 1866 the tribal delegations reluctantly submitted to the reconstruction treaties in Washington. The final treaty provided that much of the Indian land be sold or given to the government. The Seminoles surrendered their entire domain (2,170,000 acres) to the United States for fifteen cents per acre. They were to take 200,000 acres on the western border of the Creek nation, and must pay the Creeks 50 cents per acre for that land. The Creeks relinquished an additional 3,250,000 acres to the government, for which they were paid 30 cents per acre.

The Choctaw had to sell their western lands (about ¼ of the present state of Oklahoma) for the sum of $300,000. The Cherokees gave up all their lands in Southern Kansas and the rich Cherokee Strip. The federal government was to auction these lands to the white settlers and the money was to be paid to the Cherokees. In addition the Cherokees were forced to permit the government to place other tribes on certain parts of their remaining lands.

More slaves had been held by the Choctaw than by the other tribes. The treaty provided that each Negro must receive forty acres of land and be provided with a mule. And finally, all tribes were to agree to combine themselves into one government, to be known as the Indian Territory. The Indians objected most to this proposal. It was this condition that paved the way for statehood in 1907.

Judge Isaac Parker

Following the signing of the treaty the Choctaw began an attempt to reconstruct their nation according to its provisions. The new treaty had relaxed the restrictions on non-Indians entering the nation. Railroad construction crews began crisscrossing the nation, and with them came the lawless and immoral element that always accompanied the camps. The nation was rich in coal and timber. These natural resources drew investors and speculators from all over the country.

Under the terms of the treaty non-Indians could no longer be dealt with by Indian authorities, but must be tried in federal courts. Choctaw courts were to deal with all Indian offenders. The one-sided condition of this arrangement is illustrated in the fact that two of the first six men to be executed in Ft. Smith by order of the famous "hanging judge," Isaac Parker, were Indian.

Prior to the Civil War lawlessness in the Choctaw nation was at a minimum. No jails existed. When the law was violated the offender was arrested, tried, and sentenced. He was either whipped or shot, depending on the seriousness of the crime. A second offense, even in minor crimes such as theft, was almost always capital crime! The time of the execution was set some time in the future. The convicted man was free to set his house in order. There was never a case in which a full-blooded Choctaw failed to voluntarily keep his appointment with the executioner.

One of the greatest sources of trouble came from the freedmen. The national order to provide forty acres and a mule to every ex-slave in the nation drew freed Negroes from all over the South. It is estimated as many as ten thousand attempted to claim rights to this provision. No authentic records were kept of the slaves held by the Choctaw and it was difficult to disallow the claims. The Civil War had stripped the Choctaw nation of its cattle and crops. Most homes and public buildings had been destroyed. Just to secure enough food and clothing to keep alive was a major problem.

The newly arrived freedmen found life very difficult on their forty acres. Many turned to theft in order to feed their families. Complaints to the federal authorities proved fruitless. The Choctaw National Council secretly reorganized the light-horsemen and returned to them the power to sit as a court and carry out sentences on the spot. The theft of a chicken, a small pig, or grain brought the offender fifty lashes. The theft of a horse or cow, or anything of equal value, was considered a capital crime and death was the penalty. While these measures were harsh and certainly illegal under the new treaty, within months the Choctaw nation was restored to its former peaceful state.

Rev. Israel Folsom

The Cumberland Presbyterian Church in Oklahoma

In any history of the Choctaw people one is certain to come across the name of Israel Folsom. This amazing man was a full-blooded Choctaw. As a boy he shared the suffering of his people on the Trail of Tears. He was well educated and was one of the leaders who built the educational system of the Choctaw nation. He was also a historian of the Choctaw nation. His journal has provided more information about the ancient customs and religion of the Choctaw than any other source. He was a leader in tribal government and was the first Choctaw to be ordained a Cumberland Presbyterian minister.

In 1848 Israel Folsom visited the Rev. W. A. Provine, a Cumberland Presbyterian minister in Fannin County, Texas. While in Provine's home Folsom saw a copy of the Confession of Faith of the Cumberland Presbyterian Church. "Oh," he exclaimed, "I have found the church of my mother; the one in which she was converted." It is likely that Folsom's mother was converted during King and Moore's visit to the Choctaw nation in 1818. Folsom immediately requested Mr. Provine to receive him into the Cumberland Presbyterian Church. Mr. Provine asked him to wait until such time as he might visit the Choctaw country and preach to the people there.

Folsom returned home and immediately began declaring the virtues of his mother's church to his people, especially to those who were members of the Presbyterian Church, of which he himself was a member. He dwelt much on the fact that the Cumberland Presbyterian Church discarded the doctrine of fatality. This fact found much favor among the Choctaws, as they had experienced great difficulty in fitting the doctrine of fatality into their concept of God. The people told Folsom, "If you join that church, we will join too. We will go with you."

When Provine filled his appointment at the church, Israel Folsom, his wife, and ten others joined the Cumberland Presbyterian Church. One of those taking the vows was Israel's brother, Jeremiah Folsom. Israel, Jeremiah, and Solomon Archibald were already ruling elders in the Presbyterian Church. They were reinstated as ruling elders of this tiny new congregation. This was transacted on July 19, 1848, at the old "Hu-shuk-wa" church, in Blue County of the Choctaw Nation. (The name Hu-shuk-wa has no distinct meaning in Choctaw and is probably misspelled.) This was the beginning of the Cumberland Presbyterian Church in Oklahoma.

Folsom immediately began efforts to bring Cumberland Presbyterian missionaries to the Choctaw nation. He wrote to the Board many times requesting their help. In 1854 thirty-four Choctaws, including a chief, a captain, and a number of elders, sent a petition to the Board asking that they send Provine, of Texas Synod, to travel among the people of the nation for a period of one year. The petition was granted and the first Cumberland Presbyterian missionary to the new Choctaw nation began his tour of duty.

Rev. David Lowrey

In the year 1854 the Board of Missions sent the Rev. David Lowry to visit the Indian Territory and report on conditions and recommend future work among the Choctaw. Lowry had been, for many years, a missionary to the Winnebago Indians in Iowa. Lowry was much impressed with the people, and deeply moved by their desire for the gospel. He reported a need for more schools, but placed much emphasis upon the need for preaching.

At the time of Lowry's visit Israel Folsom was already an ordained minister. No date is given for the ordination, but it is quite certain he was ordained sometime in the early 1850s. Folsom's work was often interrupted by governmental responsibilities and numerous visits to Washington on behalf of his people.

From 1854 to 1906 the Board of Missions constantly sought ministers who were willing to go to the Choctaw nation. Aside from a scarcity of ministers, money was a problem. During this period some twenty men served as missionaries to the Choctaw, most of these for short periods of time. Among those serving for more lengthy periods were the Rev. R. S. Bell, the Rev. A. B. Johnson, the Rev. N. J. Crawford, and the Rev. R. C. Parks. These men were paid an average salary of $300 annually.

The merger of the Cumberland Presbyterian Church and the Presbyterian Church, U.S.A. in 1906 was a double tragedy for the churches in Choctaw Presbytery. With the loss of so many of her ministers and much property and funds, the church could no longer supply men and money for the work among the Choctaws. This loss of aid from the Board and the coming of statehood in 1907, for all practical purposes, could well have been the end of the Cumberland Presbyterian Church in Oklahoma.

However, it was at this trying time that the Indian church found strength within itself. In the attempted merger, not one minister or congregation ceased to be Cumberland Presbyterian. The great need for strong leadership produced many great men. Among these was the Rev. Henry Bond, highly educated Choctaw minister who led his people through this difficult period.

Bond was as active in state politics as he was in the church. Even today, many years after his death, when difficulty arises for the people, it is not unusual to hear the older people lament his passing and declare that if he were yet alive, the problem would be solved.

During the years from 1906 to 1945 the Board of Missions attempted to help the Choctaw churches as much as manpower and finances permitted. Of necessity this help was very limited. During this period a number of Choctaw ministers were appointed by the Board to travel in the presbytery as missionaries. Salaries for these men ranged from $200 to $300 per year to cover travel expenses. The Rev. Rayson Going, the Rev. A. G. Johnson, and the Rev. C. A. Gardner were among those carrying this responsibility. The extent of the work done by ,these men is illustrated in one of the reports of Rayson Going to the Board:

> *"In the past year I have visited in 210 homes, prayed in each, contacted 6,000 people, preached 200 sermons to 4,500 people, resulting in 30 conversions, 45 reclamations, 15 additions, baptized 8 infants and traveled 12,000 miles."*

In the mid-1940s the Board of Missions again turned its attention to the renewing of the work with the Choctaw Indians. Leadership from outside the presbytery was provided for summer camps and vacation church schools. For a short period of time some funds were made available to assist the ministers of the presbytery in travel to their churches.

In 1951 the Board appointed the Rev. Ramond Kinslow as missionary. He and his family moved to the field that same year. Kinslow found most of the church buildings in need of repair. Organization within the local churches needed strengthening and organized youth work was almost non-existent. The new missionary set to work to correct these conditions as best he could. Kinslow was well received by the people.

In 1953 the Rev. John Lovelace was appointed missionary and sent to Choctaw Presytery to help in the work. Lovelace served as pastor of one Indian, Wright City, and one non-Indian church, Honey Grove, in the presbytery. In addition to pastoral duties he assisted Kinslow in the general work of the presbytery. At the resignation of Mr. Kinslow in 1954, Mr. Lovelace continued as the only missionary to the Choctaws.

During Lovelace's tenure as missionary a manse was built in Idabel for the missionary and his family. Funds for the manse were raised through the children's mission project across the church. The Honey Grove church building was constructed while Mr. Lovelace was missionary. The Oak Hill congregation (non-Indian) was organized and a building erected.

In 1959 Lovelace left the work in Choctaw Presbytery to serve as missionary in Colombia, S.A. The Rev. Charles Faith was appointed missionary to Choctaw Presbytery.

During the time Mr. Faith served, much organizational work was done in the Indian churches. Youth groups were organized, women's missionary auxiliaries and men's fellowships were organized and strengthened, the rally and camping program was expanded. Faith organized a missionary fellowship (non-Indian) in the Pine Lake community, near Broken Bow. This fellowship was later organized as the Pine Lake Cumberland Presbyterian Church.

Faith resigned as missionary in the winter of 1964. The Rev. Claude Gilbert, then pastor of the Honey Grove and Oak Hill churches in Choctaw Presbytery, was named missionary by the Board of Missions.

Choctaw Presbytery Today[2]

Today there are fourteen active churches in Choctaw Presbytery. Three of these are non-Indian congregations: Honey Grove, Oak Hill, Pine Lake. The newest church is Pine Lake which was organized February 4, 1967. All the churches are located in rural areas. Some of the Indian churches are as much as forty miles from the nearest town.

Choctaw Presbytery covers twelve counties in Southeastern Oklahoma with the churches scattered evenly over this large area. The boundaries of the presbytery follow the boundaries of the Choctaw nation at the end of the Civil War. There are no reservations in Oklahoma. The people are free to move about and to travel where they like.

The churches of Choctaw Presbytery minister to about one thousand people regularly. Of this number only about three hundred are members of the Cumberland Presbyterian Church. The remainder hold membership in the United Presbyterian Church, U.S.A., Presbyterian Church, U.S., and the United Methodist Church. While holding membership in these churches, many people participate fully in the Cumberland Presbyterian program, sharing in the responsibility and the financial obligations of the congregations. It is a rare

---

[2]Rev. Gilbert wrote in 1968. Since that time all of the Anglo churches that were in Choctaw presbytery have closed.

thing for the Choctaw to change his official church affiliation. Even though he might worship and work for years with another congregation, he normally retains his traditional church membership.

The Cumberland Presbyterian Church is the only denomination that provides a full-time missionary to the Choctaw. The United Presbyterian Church and the Presbyterian Church, U.S. provide some guidance through the synodical church extension boards. This guidance is limited due to other responsibilities within their synods, and the fact that these men are not residents of the area. It is the announced policy of the United Presbyterian Church and Presbyterian Church, U.S. to work toward integrating the Indian churches into the non-Indian congregations of the area. The Indian people are strongly opposed to this policy.

The United Methodist Church continues a policy of relying on native leadership in Indian churches. This would be a sound policy, except for the fact there is no trained native leadership available. Most Methodist Indian churches are served by lay preachers. For these reasons more and more of the people are turning to the Cumberland Presbyterian Church for spiritual fulfillment.

The program of Choctaw Presbytery is an ambitious one, and not always carried through to a satisfactory conclusion. The planning must provide for the needs of young people who face every problem of contemporary life, plus added frustrations derived through Indian culture and background. At the same time provision must be made for the older people whose customs and desires must be respected.

Four rallies are held each year. These meetings start on Friday evening and conclude on Sunday afternoon. It would be a mistake to consider these meetings as "youth rallies" because all ages actively participate. The program includes classes and activities for all ages. A presbyterial camp is held each year. This too is a family affair, with everyone taking part.

Spring presbytery starts on Thursday and concludes Saturday night. Again, every one is present. The fall meeting of Presbytery requires but two days. In most cases everyone stays at the church through Sunday, following presbytery, for worship and visiting.

A five-day vacation church school is conducted at each of the churches annually. Some VCS leadership is provided from outside the presbytery, usually two students. Additional staff is chosen from among local people. This includes the pastor, his wife, and any others who might be persuaded to help. Vacation church school enrollment in the presbytery varies from three hundred to five hundred.

Much has been said of the poor stewardship practices of the Choctaw congregations. The official statistics would seem to bear out this observation. However, we must consider the extreme poverty in this area. The per capita income of the Choctaw ranks among the lowest in the United States. Even so, as stewards, the Choctaw would put many Cumberland Presbyterians to shame. For example, all meetings are held at the local churches. The host church provides for all the needs of the people while they are there. Often as many as two hundred will attend meetings lasting a week. Food alone will cost several hundred dollars. This expense is shared by the fifteen to twenty people of the host church.

In addition to the outlay of cash, the local women prepare and serve the food and provide bedding for all the visitors. The men slaughter hogs, gather wood, and carry water. It is not unusual for the host congregation to borrow money to have the meeting and then struggle for months paying it back. A similar procedure is followed in rallies, camps, meetings of presbytery, and the vacation church schools. The churches are very much concerned for the mission work of the denomination, and make an admirable contribution in that area. The Choctaw, as a Christian steward, need not be ashamed.

There are six active ministers in Choctaw Presbytery—five Indian ministers and the missionary. In addition there are four retired ministers who, because of their age, are unable to serve the churches. Each of the active ministers serves two or three churches, and in some instances drives as far as 150 miles to his appointments. The ministers' cars are all old and breakdowns are frequent. Usually they take their families with them.

Services at the Indian churches normally start on Saturday and continue through Sunday evening. In 1967 the average salary of the Indian minister was less than $200 per year. In most cases their transportation cost was greater than the total amount they received.

The missionary serves the three white congregations and serves as supply pastor of the McGee Chapel church, an Indian church without a pastor. The missionary gives direction to all the work in the presbytery, directing the camps, rallies, and vacation church schools. He attempts to aid in government programs affecting the Indian people, counsels the young people in educational planning, and in general offers all available assistance possible to the needs of the people.

Regular visits by the missionary to the Indian churches are scheduled on Wednesday evenings. He conducts services at each of the three non-Indian churches on Sundays. At the Wednesday meetings the missionary meets with the session, the youth groups, the CPW, or with any group at requests his assistance. He conducts a worship service, plans .building repairs, or assists with any problem facing the congregation.

Future Needs of the Choctaw

The continuing needs of the Indian churches remain much as they have been in the past: trained leadership; adequate buildings for worship and study; facilities for the extensive camping program carried out in the presbytery. Education of the young people past the high school level is greatly needed and perhaps, more than anything else, all need the patience and understanding of the church of which they are a part.

Steps are being taken to fill these needs. In 1968 two new church buildings were constructed. One is at Lone Star and the other is at Gum Creek. These buildings cost $3,500 and $4,000 respectively. The funds for this construction were borrowed from the denominational Board of Finance and will be repaid in monthly installments by the congregations. This is by far the greatest financial obligation ever undertaken by an Indian congregation.

Today more Choctaw young people are entering college or technical school than a any time in this century. In 1960 only 12% those finishing high school continued in some kind of higher education. In 1967, 30% of the graduating young people are continuing their education.

The denominational Board of Missions has purchased land in Coctaw Presbytery as a site for a permanent camp. Money is being raised through the children's mission project in 1967, 1968, and 1969 for the construction of a dining hall, cabins, class areas and recreation facilities. A well and bath houses will be provided. This camp will be used for rallies, summer camp, meetings of presbytery, family retreats, leadership workshops, and ministerial training. In addition the facility will be made available to other church groups who have need of it especially to those churches serving Indian people.

It is difficult for those outside the presbytery to understand the pressing need for this facility. At present all gatherings are held at the Indian churches. The church buildings are all small and several are no larger than 14' x 25'. Most of the churches are located in remote areas. Cooking is done in camp houses, only partially enclosed, and food is often served outside. An adequate water supply is not available and sanitation facilities are non-existent.

The people are convinced of the value of religious instruction especially for the children. So convinced are they, in fact, that they have been willing to make the necessary sacrifices and endure the hardships imposed by these conditions. They are willing to continue with what is available if necessary. However, the matter is being taken out of their hands. State laws which forbid overnight camping by large numbers of people where sanitation facilities are not provided are now being enforced. The new Choctaw camp will insure the continuation of the effective youth work of the past years.

As to the final need—that of patience and understanding—this is the purpose of this narrative. To understand and to appreciate the Choctaw one must know something of what he is, and why he is that way. To know this we must know something of his history, his heritage, and his customs. It is necessary to try to put oneself in his place and to look back over the years of injustice, to see his golden years also—the years of success and dignity. We should recognize his potential, his love for his people, the close kinship that exists among the Choctaw; see his pride and at the same time his humility; see his faith and his love for the church; see his desire and his hope to again become a great people. Only then can we hope to understand the Choctaw, and when we understand him we will want to help him accomplish his goals.

It is an easy matter to shrug off past injustices to the Indian by saying he is simply a victim of progress. In reality it was not progress that drove the people from their homes in Mississippi; it was greed . It was not progress that slaughtered them on the "death march" .to the new country; it was greed. It was not progress but greed that violated treaties and imposed unnecessary and inhuman hardships following the Civil War. It was not progress that finally wrested their last remaining possession from them; it was the greed of a nation of land hungry, self-centered intruders.

But what have we to do with this? We did not drive them out, or take their land. Perhaps our fathers did, but not we. If this had happened m our day, would we not have handled it differently? Our Lord commented on just such a situation:

> *"you say . . . 'If we had lived in the days of our fathers, we would not have taken part with them in shedding the blood of .the prophets.' Thus you witness against yourselves, that you are sons of those who murdered the prophets. Fill up, then, the measure of your fathers."* (Matthew 23:30-32).

Acknowledgments:

Time and memory will not permit a complete bibliography. Some of the sources of information used in the manuscript are listed here. Much of the material comes from my notes collected over a period of several years.

A History of the American Indians, H. B. Cushman.
A History of the Cumberland Presbyterian Church, B. W. McDonnald
North American Indians, George Catlin
Oklahoma, A History of Five Centuries, Arrell M. Gibson
Oklahoma, Daisy L. Moore
Removal of the Mississippi Choctaws, John W. Wade
The Social and Ceremonial Life of the Choctaw Indians, John R. Swanton
The Work of the Cumberland Presbyterian Church With the Choctaw Indians, John Lovelace

—CLAUDE GILBERT

REV. ROBERT BELL
(1810-1853)
by Richard Beard

Sources: Rev. C.H. Bell, D.D.; Smith's **History of the Cumberland Presbyterians**, **Banner of Peace**.

Robert Bell was born in Guilford county, North Carolina, December 16, 1770. His father's name was Robert; his mother's family-name was Walker. He had but one full brother. This brother was the father of the Hon. John Bell, of Tennessee. There were several full sisters, besides a number of half brothers and sisters.

When he was twelve years old his father moved to the Cumberland country. The first settlement of the family was north of Cumberland River, in what is now Sumner county. In a year or two they moved to the neighborhood of what is now Nashville, and settled there.

At some time early in the revival of 1800 he made profession of religion. The exact time, however, is not known. At the sessions of the Transylvania Presbytery, in October of 1802, Mr. Bell was licensed as an exhorter and catechist. At the same Presbytery Hugh Kirkpatrick and Ephraim McLean were received as candidates for the ministry. At some time between the fall of 1802 and December of 1805 he was received as a candidate for the ministry, and licensed as a probationer. This is inferred from the fact that, in the proceedings of the Commission of the Synod of Kentucky, which met early in December, 1805, he is recognized as a licensed probationer, and was one of those who were forbidden to exercise any ministerial functions derived from the authority of the Cumberland Presbytery. The licentiates and exhorters were included in the prohibition.

It is supposed that his education was perhaps better than that of most of the young men of his time who came into the ministry, but its extent cannot be distinctly stated. The probability is, that it was irregularly acquired, as the circumstances of the country would allow, and as his own disposition would prompt. A man of his habits of mind would be apt to make the most of his circumstances in the way of improving himself. It is certain that, by his own application, after he entered the ministry he became a good English and Latin scholar.

It is said, upon his own authority, that when the Commission of Synod was in session, considering the cases of the young men, he was privately approached, and assured that if he would adopt the Confession of Faith without reservation, his license as a probationer for the ministry would be continued. He, however, declined the proposition.

It appears from the history of the proceedings of the Commission that when the question of submission to a reexamination was put to the young men individually, he and Samuel K. Blythe, a candidate for the ministry, "requested a short time to consider the subject." No one who knew the character of Mr. Bell would be surprised at the request on his part. He was an unusually thoughtful and conscientious man. The result of the consideration was that both the men refused to submit, as did all the others. The ground of the refusal was a constitutional one. It was, "That they believed the Cumberland Presbytery was a regular judicature of the Church, and competent to judge of the faith and ability of its candidates; that they themselves had not been charged with heresy or immorality—and if they had been, the Presbytery would have been the proper judicature to call them to account." The question was, as I have said, a constitutional one, and the young men were clearly justifiable in their refusal. The proceedings of the Commission were obviously unconstitutional and anti-Presbyterian. The New Brunswick Presbytery had taken the same view of the subject more then half a century before.

  The same difficulties were in the way of Mr. Bell's advancement in the ministry, which were in the way of others. The action of the Commission left the Presbytery in a state of confusion. Nothing was done presbyterially until after the organization in 1810. We have nothing official on the subject, but Mr. Donnell says that he was licensed in 1804, and ordained in 1810. His ordination appears, therefore, to have been one among the first Presbyterial acts of the new Presbytery.

From his licensure in 1804 to 1807 he lived in Logan county, Kentucky, and his labors were partially, at least, confined to that section of country. In 1807 he moved to Bean's Creek, near Salem, Tennessee, and settled there.

In the Minutes of the old Cumberland Synod, which met on the 19th of October, 1819, at Suggs's Creek Meeting-house, in Wilson county, Tennessee, we have the following record:

> Whereas several letters have been directed to the Moderator informing the Synod that a number of societies have been formed, the object of which is to raise funds for the purpose of establishing schools for the literary and religious instruction of the Chickasaw and Choctaw Tribes of Indians, and appointing the ordained ministers of this Synod their Board of Trustees; therefore,
>
> Resolved, That this appointment be accepted.

This preamble and resolution is the first public indication of a measure which, in its time, attracted a great deal of attention in the Church. Mr. Bell, too, spent some of the best years of his life in efforts for its promotion. A sort of spontaneous feeling began to develop itself in different parts of the Church in favor of endeavoring to civilize and Christianize the Southern Indians. The Creek war had passed over, and the Chickasaws and Choctaws had maintained such relations to the whites during that struggle that a favorable public attention was naturally directed to them.

From the report on the state of religion to the Synod at its sessions in the same year I make the following extract relating to this subject:

> By the heaven-born charity and zeal of some female members of the Church, funds have been raised, which have enabled the Missionary Board to employ several missionaries a considerable part of their time, by which your bounds have been much enlarged in the South and West. This has multiplied the calls and cries to our Presbyteries and Missionary Boards for help. The people desire the word and ordinances. Among the most impressive calls we hear is one from the tawny sons of the woods in the South. One of them has recently given satisfactory evidence that he has obtained the 'one thing needful,' and he has been admitted to the sealing ordinances of the Church.
>
> This Indian man was brought from the Chickasaw Nation of Indians last winter by Revs. Samuel King and William Moore, two of our missionaries. He has been boarding with Brother King, and going to school from his house, and has made almost unparalleled progress in his education. Your committee anticipate great good to his nation from his

education and conversion, especially if it should please the great Head of the Church to call him to the work of the ministry.

It seems that, in consequence of the opening condition of things, and the state of feeling developed in the Church, the plan was conceived of a school in the Chickasaw Nation which should combine at once instruction in letters and religion, together with domestic, agricultural, and mechanical pursuits.

Accordingly, on the 11th of September, 1820, the following articles of an agreement were entered into by Revs. Samuel King, Robert Bell, and James Stewart, as the representatives of the Cumberland Presbyterian Board of Missions, which consisted of the ordained ministers of the Cumberland Presbyterian Church on the one part, and the chiefs of the Chickasaw Nation on the other part:

> Articles of Agreement between Samuel King, James Stewart, and Robert Bell, missionaries, and the chiefs of the Chickasaw Nation, viz.:
> Article 1. We, the said Samuel King, James Stewart, and Robert Bell, on the part of the Board of the Cumberland Presbyterian Missionary Society, do promise to teach the people of the said nation reading, writing, and arithmetic, and a knowledge of agriculture and the mechanical arts. Also those who resort to

them for instruction shall be boarded and clothed gratuitously, provided they are not able to clothe themselves.

Article 2. We promise that we will not take more land than will be necessary for the support of the institution. And should we leave the institution, the houses and land which we have occupied shall revert to the Indians.

Article 3. We, the chiefs of the Chickasaw Nation, on the part of said nation, do permit said society and missionaries to come into our nation to teach our young people.

Article 4. We do hereby bind ourselves to allow said society as much land as may be necessary for the support of their missionaries, which land they shall hold as long as they continue to teach our children.

Sept. 11, 1820.

These articles were signed by Messrs. King, Stewart, and Bell, on the part of the Missionary Board; and on the part of the Chickasaws, by Stako Tookey, King of the Nation; and Tisho Mingo, Appa Suntubba, Samuel Sealy, William McGelbra, James Colbert, and Levi Colbert, chiefs.

In the month of November a school was opened, under the name of Charity Hall, within the limits of what is now the State of Mississippi, about seven miles from the present city of Aberdeen, and three miles from Cotton Gin Port. Mr. Bell was appointed superintendent. He taught a few weeks in a private room furnished by one of the chiefs until suitable buildings were prepared for the use of the school. The buildings erected were plain and cheap, costing in all about $1,500. Thirty acres of land were cleared, and put under cultivation. The Indians learned with some facility, and labored with as much readiness as would have been expected. The Government of the United States contributed liberally toward paying for the buildings, and also made an annual contribution of $300 or $400 toward keeping up the school. But great difficulties were experienced in carrying forward the work. Mr. Bell, in his communications, complains especially of the depreciation of the currency in those parts of the Church from which he received his principal supplies. Of course a great many members of the Church were indifferent toward the enterprise. Some were even opposed to it. There were lingering prejudices against the Indians. Still great efforts were made. Many of the preachers and people cooperated earnestly with the good man in the work upon which his heart was deeply set. I have before me files of subscriptions of money from men and women scattered all over the Church—subscriptions ranging from ten dollars to twenty-five cents—also of clothing, from a jeans coat to a pair of socks.

I transcribe a copy of one of the appeals to the Church. It is from William Harris, who never spoke otherwise than earnestly on such a subject:

Friends, who have felt the sweets of learning and religion, suffer a call to be made on the benevolence of your hearts in behalf of the poor heathen children of the Chickasaw Nation now under the care of the Cumberland Presbyterian Missionary Board at Charity Hall School. Will you aid in bringing them from under the gloom of heathen darkness by giving some of the abundance with which you have been blessed, in money, school-books, or country-cloth suitable to clothe the naked children of the woods? Any thing of the kind will be thankfully received by

WILLIAM HARRIS,
Agent for Logan Presbytery.
May 17, 1825.

Notwithstanding these efforts the enterprise dragged heavily. Some of my first recollections of the old Cumberland Synod, which commenced in 1822, are recollections of troubles and discouragements connected with Charity Hall. My feelings at those times were, and they still are, that Mr. Bell's patience, and perseverance, and Christian forbearance, under all the trials arising out of his situation, were almost superhuman. The trials were very great. One thing has affected me much in examining the old papers relating to Charity Hall. I allude to the respectful consideration in all transactions with the Federal Government with which he was treated by its officers. There are repeated communications from Hon. John C. Calhoun, a portion of the time Secretary of War; from Hon. John B. McKinney; and again from Hon. William B. Lewis, as well as others. Every intimation in every communication indicates that they consider themselves communicating with a high-minded, honorable, Christian man. Whilst his brethren were sometimes impatient and fretful, not always fully respectful, and sometimes fault-finding, there is no intimation of the kind from these high government officials. Mr. Bell's descendants and the Church which he so nobly represented through all these years of trial ought to regard such testimony from such a quarter, although indirect, as an imperishable treasure.

The Synod were in the habit, from year to year, of appointing a commission of their own body to visit Charity Hall, and make report of its condition, system of operations, and general prospects. I transcribe here one of those reports as an illustration of the general operations and prospects of the school. The Commission on this occasion consisted of Revs. James S. Guthrie, David Foster, and James Stewart. Mr. Stewart did not attend. Messrs. Foster and Guthrie report the following:

> According to the appointment of the Cumberland Presbyterian Missionary Board, David Foster and James S. Guthrie met at Charity Hall Missionary Establishment, Chickasaw Nation, on Friday, the 20th of

May, 1825. James Stewart was absent.

THE STATE OF RELIGION AT THE ESTABLISHMENT

On Friday evening after the arrival of your committee we had preaching. On Saturday two discourses were delivered, and, toward the close, the little congregation manifested great solemnity and deep concern—tears were flowing, and six or eight came forward for prayer, one or two being Indians. About as many were whites, and the remainder were blacks.

On Sabbath, after preaching, the ordinance of the Lord's Supper was administered, at which your committee were rejoiced to see some of the first-fruits of missionary labor in the Chickasaw Nation seated at the Lord's table. At the evening preaching a considerable company collected. They received the word of life with more than ordinary interest; many wept; some came to join in public prayer, and it is hoped that one black woman raised in the nation found peace with God. About four connected themselves with the Mission Church as seekers of religion. Your committee are sorry to say that some of the Chickasaws, both male and female, who, as they are informed, had appeared to be deeply concerned, were during the occasion but little affected, though others appeared anxious to know and understand what was done on the occasion. Upon the whole, your committee think the prospect of religion to be flattering about the establishment, and particularly so among the black people, who are much concerned about the state of their souls, through the nation, as far as they had information. The black people generally can speak and understand English, and this your committee think to be the reason why they feel more interest about religion than the Indians. It is but just to observe that the black people in this nation have less extravagance connected with their religious feelings than the committee have witnessed in other places. During preaching, many of the Indians seemed inattentive and restless, though not as much so as we frequently find among the white people. The Indians view the white people as their superiors, and it is probable that their example has its influence with the Indians.

After describing the locality and appurtenances of the farm, the report proceeds to the

STATE OF THE SCHOOL.

The school consists of thirty scholars, who attend, in general, regularly. A few, however, are not perfectly regular in their attendance. We heard a small class of beginners spell in two syllables, and a larger class spell in different places in the book. when the words were given out, the little fellows seemed ready to catch the sound, and apply suitable letters, though they sometimes missed the spelling of the word. Others, however, who were farther advanced, never missed the spelling of a single word, though the words were selected from different tables in the book. The small class in the New Testament read imperfectly, though we think, for the time they have spent, they are in a good way of improvement. The next Testament class read well, yet all read too low.

The class in the English Reader read very correctly. They all appeared to understand the Key to Webster's Spelling-book.

Two are studying English Grammar who have begun to parse. It does not appear that they will improve in grammar as rapidly as in spelling, reading, and writing. We observed no symptoms of quarreling among the scholars, nor of doing mischief to one another, as we frequently find in schools among the whites. They appeared, however, full of mirth and play, and this we were informed was generally the case.

GENERAL RULES

About day-light the trumpet is blown—the signal for all to rise. In half an hour it is blown again, that all may attend family-worship in the dining-room. Within five minutes from the close of the worship,

Mr. Bell, with the boys, repairs to the field until eight or nine o'clock, and Mrs. Bell, with the girls, to sewing or other employments. They are then called to breakfast, where Mr. Bell is seated at the head of the table, with the boys on one side and the girls on the other. When breakfast is over, they repair to school until twelve o'clock. After an interval of an hour, they are called by the trumpet to dinner. After dinner, until four o'clock, they are at school. They then go to the field until night, when all are called to supper and family--worship. Throughout the whole, the scholars appear to be under strict discipline, which they observe with promptness and cheerfulness, except that they seem a little slow to start to work in the morning, but when at work they seem brisk and cheerful.

REMARKS

Mr. and Mrs. Bell have more labor to perform, and more business of different kinds upon their hands by far than they should have. They have more to do than they can do in justice either to themselves or to the interest of the establishment, and unless they have some assistance in future, their days must certainly be shortened. We hope and believe, however, from various indications, that the needed assistance will be supplied, and that measure will be vigorously prosecuted to make the school a blessing to the nation, and a means of salvation to hundreds of poor Indians.

I omit a part of this report because of its length, but have embodied what I present here for three reasons.

First. The source from which it comes makes it reliable. I knew the men most intimately, and have no doubt that in every statement they were faithful. There is no varnishing in the document.

Secondly. It sets forth something of the labors and self-denial of Mr. Bell. In 1825 he was fifty-five years old, and yet we find him in the field at work with the Indian boys, and in the school-room teaching dull children the spelling-book and the English Reader, whilst his wife, of corresponding age, is endeavoring to indoctrinate the Indian girls into the mysteries of spinning, and sewing, and weaving, and cooking. And the committee say, they are wearing themselves out at this work.

Thirdly. It will be useful to the present and succeeding generations of members of this Church to know something of what their fathers and mothers have done and suffered. Fifty years ago the Cumberland Presbyterian Church had a Foreign Mission, and although they perhaps did not discharge their whole duty toward it, still they were sustaining it. How far have we advanced in that direction in these fifty years? The committee mention in this report a fact which I have omitted—the loss of a beloved son on the part of these old people at the Mission. This son most likely fell a victim to a sickly climate and locality. Yet the parents labored on. There are a few men in the Church, and but a few, who, with myself, will recollect the intense and undying interest which Mr. Bell manifested on all suitable occasions in the prosperity of the Mission. He evidently felt his work there to be the great work of his life. Nor was all this labor lost. Without doubt there was seed sown at Charity Hall which will bring forth fruit forever.

The last report on file from Mr. Bell, as superintendent of the Mission, was made in 1830. This report was made to the Cumberland Board of Missions, or rather at that time to the General Assembly. There is a copy of a document transmitted to the General Government in 1832. This is the latest document which I find on file. About this time the removal of the Indians to their present locality became a subject of agitation. This, of course, would unsettle every thing connected with the Mission. The actual removal of the Indians at last is a subject for the national historian. In some of its aspects it will be a dark chapter in our record.

After the close of the Mission-school, Mr. Bell settled in the interior of Mississippi, in what is now Pontotoc county. The last twenty years of his life were devoted earnestly and laboriously to preaching the gospel. His labors ended only with his life. On the 9th of November, 1853, this life came to an end. He died in his eighty-third year. He had an appointment for preaching the Sabbath previous to his death. Being upon his death-bed, he was, of course, unable to fill it, and it was filled by his grandson, Rev. C. H. Bell, now of Oxford, Mississippi. After the return of young Mr. Bell, the old man inquired particularly about the meeting, indicating still an unflagging interest in the welfare of the Church and the salvation of his fellow-men.

Mr. Bell married, some time in the earlier part of his life, a Miss Grizzell McCutcheon, of Logan county, Kentucky. They had four children—two sons and two daughters. The younger son died at Charity Hall, or while his parents were connected with the Mission-school. The event has been already mentioned. The other son was the late General John Bell, of Mississippi. The daughters still live—one in Mississippi, the other in Texas. The latter is the wife of Rev. John Haynes, of Pilot Point, Texas.

Says a correspondent:

> Mr. Bell was a great man; great because he was faithful and good—good so far as it may be said that a mere man is good. He loved the gospel, loved the Church, loved the souls of men, and was himself universally beloved. 'An excellent spirit was in him.' He was characteristically modest and retiring in his habits. It is perhaps not proper to say that a man can be too modest, otherwise I should say he was too much so. He was remarkably conscientious, even scrupulous, in the observance of the Sabbath. He prepared for the day

of rest, and required others of his household to do the same. He was not rich, but God in his providence had favored him, and he was in what would be called independent circumstances.

At a meeting of the Presbytery to which he belonged, two or three weeks before his death, he seemed to be under the impression that it would be his last Presbyterial meeting on earth. An order was passed for the ordination of his grandson. The young man hesitated, but his reluctance was overcome by the obvious anxiety of the grandfather that the ordination should be consummated, and his own apprehension that it would be the old man's last meeting with the Presbytery. The ordination proceeded, and the aged patriarch participated. Never shall I forget his noble, venerable, and benevolent countenance: how it beamed with joy while he participated in the solemnities of the occasion. It seemed as though one of the fathers of apostolic times had come down among us. O that the grandson may be as good, as holy, and as devoted as his predecessor?

His domestic relations were of the happiest kind. Not long before his death he remarked to a circle of friends, in the presence of his wife, that "they had lived together fifty-four years, and no unkind word had ever passed between them." She was a few years his junior, and survived him about six months.

Mention has been made of the extent of Mr. Bell's early education. Of course, but little is known on this subject. But Rev. Dr. C. H. Bell, of Mississippi, says: "He was a close student through life, and a careful reader even in his old age. On his death-bed he gave me his copy of Scott's Commentary, in five volumes, with Cruden's Concordance, to correspond with it. The Commentary is marked throughout with his pencil." The pencil marks are the indications of close reading.

I copy the following letter from the Banner of Peace, of December 15, 1853. It is from Rev. Robert Donnell:

ANOTHER OF THE FATHERS OF THE CUMBERLAND PRESBYTERIAN CHURCH GONE TO HIS REWARD.

ATHENS, ALA., November 23, 1853.

MESSRS. EDITORS:—The Rev. Robert Bell, near Pontotoc, Mississippi, departed this life on the 9th of October, in the eighty-third year of his age. He was a subject of the revival of 1800. He was received as a candidate for the ministry soon after Anderson, Ewing, and King. He was licensed about 1804, and ordained in 1810. The delay of his ordination was produced by the protracted difficulties with the Mother Church. Through that whole struggle he was firm and prayerful.

No one labored harder to promote religion, and no one was more rejoiced to hear of the organization of the Cumberland Presbytery by McAdow, Ewing, and King, than Brother Bell.

He was a man of retiring modesty, sound sense, and humble deportment, and was untiring in his efforts to do good. His fidelity would not suffer him to impose on others, and his prudence prevented others from imposing on him. He was firm, but not obstinate; he was humble, but not mean; he thought for himself, but was cheerful in allowing others to think for themselves. He was contemporary with the great and good men, McGready, Hodge, McGee, McAdow, Ewing, and King, as well as younger brethren in the ministry. He planted many churches, and fed the flock over which the Holy Ghost had made him overseer. He was an indulgent master, a kind father, an affectionate husband, a consistent Christian, and a devoted minister of Jesus Christ. He lived long; he labored hard to the last, a when on his bed of death, had an appointment out which a grandson, at his request, filled. May the mantle of the grandfather remain on that son, who, by the trembling hand of a grandfather, with others, had just been set apart to the whole work of the ministry of the gospel! Were I able to write, I would move, if I could, the whole Cumberland Presbyterian Church, especially its ministry, by his example, to redoubled diligence in the cause of God. The

Church, of which he was a member, was raised up to aid other Christian Churches in hastening on the latter-day glory. We have no time to idle away, no Sabbaths to spend without preaching. A minister's call is for life. Old ministers, like old David, want to show to the present generation, and to every one that is to come, the power and glory of God.

I would say to his congregations, He has left you a minister of his own family. To his family I would say, Trust in the lord, and he will be to you a father that will never die. To his aged and Christian companion, I would say, Your husband, in all your removals, has been the pioneer, and he has gone before you now, to prepare, or see first, the place prepared for you, and until you are called home—to your happy home—your strength shall be equal to your day. With your departed husband, you have borne the burden and heat of the day. Your reward shall be as his; he had gone first, but you will not be long behind him. It must have been consoling to him, and to you both, to see the Church, for which you have labored so long, in a prosperous state.

Brother Bell was emphatically one of the fathers of the Cumberland Presbyterian Church. I have been indisposed for some time, and am not now able to write. Those capable, and who have promised a history of the fathers of the Church, will give a full history.

Brothers Kirkpatrick,[3] Porter, Calhoon, and McSpadden are on the list before me—on the list of the ministry-but I may be first on the list of mortality. May we all depart out of this world as tranquilly as Brother Bell, and all the fathers of the Church who have gone!

R. DONNELL.

The following is a copy of a letter addressed to Rev. Robert Donnell, by the surviving son of Mr. Bell, in relation to his father's death. It was published in the Banner of Peace, of January 12, 1854. Every thing on the subject is interesting:

REV. AND DEAR FRIEND:—In father's death, all his children, and relations, and friends that were around him feel a great bereavement. They are consoled alone from the fact of his great resignation, his patient endurance of his affliction and suffering, and the undisturbed sereneness of his mind in his

---

[3]Rev. Hugh Kirkpatrick was born in Orleans county, North Carolina, May 8, 1774, and was brought up in the Presbyterian Church. He married Isabella Stewart, of the same county and State, July 2, 1795. Both professed religion in 1797, and soon emigrated to the South-west, spent one year in Kentucky, but finally settled in Sumner county, Tennessee. They were two of the first four that joined the Beech Congregation. He was licensed to preach by the Transylvania Presbytery at its sessions in October, 1803. His education was better than that of the ordinary young men, as they were called. After 1805, he followed the fortunes of the Council, and was one of the first who was ordained after the organization of Cumberland Presbytery in 1810. He was a good man, and spent the most of his life and ministry in Sumner county. His wife died in 1859, and in his old age he married Nancy Grizzard. He died in 1863, leaving an only son, who still survives him.

dying hour; and from the reflection that he has made, we doubt not, a happy exchange of bodily suffering for that unalloyed happiness which we most confidently believe is to be the reward of a long life devoted diligently, faithfully, and continually, down to his last moments, to the service of Him who promises to reward the good and faithful servant. Few die as he did. He had prayed for dying grace, and it was given him. He breathed out his life without a struggle, or a groan, or the distortion of a muscle of his face, perfectly in his senses, closing his own eyes and his own mouth, leaving a serene and smiling expression upon his face which he took with him to the grave. Better evidence of a full preparation for death could not have been afforded, and it is sinful in us, perhaps, to lament our bereavement.

Father, for a good many years, was afflicted with rheumatic pains in both his hip-joints, also with asthma, and considerable nervousness, especially in his right arm and hand. Of this you are, perhaps, aware; otherwise his health was generally good. For a long time he was unable to ride on horseback, but with the aid of a staff he could walk about. In riding he used his buggy; and, for several months before his death, to enable himself to walk, he had frequently to use two staves.

Although his voice had become very weak, he continued to preach nearly every Sabbath up to the time he was taken down; but, standing in the pulpit, to preach even a short sermon, fatigued him very much, and often after preaching, on account of his asthmatic affection, he would have great difficulty in breathing. For many years, on account of the nervousness in his right arm and hand, he was compelled to write with his left hand.

The attack of sickness of which he died arose evidently from exposure and cold, which brought on what is called here typhoid pneumonia. The Presbytery to which he belonged sat at the church, where he preached to the congregation under his care, near his home. The Presbytery met on the third Friday in September, and, contrary to advice, he would attend the meetings day and night until it closed. In the meantime a change of weather took place, and the nights became cool. He was up several nights until after midnight. The cold he contracted at this meeting was no doubt the occasion of his death. He was taken sick on Friday, after the adjournment of the Presbytery, and lived seventeen days after he was taken down. Having had frequent attacks of a similar kind, and from the same cause, and attended with more pain—for he did not complain of much suffering, his cough being the worst—he indulged the belief that he would recover until the evening before his death. For more than a week, however, he was well aware that his case was a critical one, and always expressed himself with perfect resignation to the will of Providence in regard to him. He died on Sunday, and on that day he was to have preached the funeral-sermon of an old revolutionary soldier, who had died a few weeks previously, and who had requested that father should perform that service. Although unable to fulfill the engagement, he kept it in mind to the last. Also the morning before he died he urged my son, who did not wish to leave him, to fill his place at one of his stated appointments for preaching about three miles off, and when my son returned and reported to him that he had done so, it seemed to relieve and satisfy him. His whole mind appeared to be absorbed in the interests of religion, giving himself little concern about the things of this world.

Before leaving this branch of the subject I cannot refrain from relating an incident or two which took place during the sessions of the Presbytery. On account of his infirmity, father petitioned the Presbytery to release him from the pastoral charge of the Church which had been under his care ever since he had been living here, which, I believe, was not granted. At the same Presbytery the ordination of my son, Claibourne, took place. I was not present, but it was said that the scene was an unusually interesting one, and that the whole congregation was bathed in tears. When it came to the laying on of hands, and when my old father came tottering forward, supported by his staff, to lay his weak and trembling hand upon the head of his grandson, a deep and solemn sensation was produced. All felt that his work was about done, and that this would be perhaps the last ministerial act of his life. It seemed a transfer of his mantle to a younger branch of the family for continuing and carrying on the good work in which he had been so long engaged.

Of father's early history, and particularly from the time he engaged in the ministry, I suppose you are rather well acquainted. He was born, I think, in North Carolina, and I have often heard him say that he was nine years old when the battle of Guilford was fought in that State, and that his father lived nine miles from that place at the time. About the year 1784 or 1785, when he was fourteen or fifteen years old, his father moved to the Cumberland country, and settled near Nashville. This was in the midst of the troublesome times with the Indians, against whom my father, with others, made several excursions. In 1795 he married, and moved to the State of Kentucky, and settled in Logan county. About the year 1804 or 1805 he commenced the ministry as a circuit-rider. In the fall of 1806 he moved back to Tennessee and settled in Franklin county; and in 1820 he moved to the Chickasaw Nation, and engaged in the missionary work among the Chickasaw Indians under the patronage of the Cumberland Presbyterian Church. He continued in that business until about the year 1830 or 1831. In 1836 he settled a few miles from Pontotoc, Mississippi, where he spent the remainder of his days. It appears from the record of his age that he was born on the 16th of December, 1770. Consequently, had he lived to the 16th of December next, he would have completed eighty-three years. Your sincere friend and relative,

JOHN BELL

My personal knowledge of Mr. Bell was very limited. I never heard him preach but once. In 1817, in the month of October, I attended a camp-meeting at the Beech Meeting-house, a place frequently mentioned in these "Brief Sketches." I had professed religion but a few weeks before. Mr. Bell was at that meeting, and preached on Sabbath. He was then, of course, in the prime of life. I recollect his appearance very distinctly. He was well dressed, and had altogether a gentlemanly aspect. His text was: "Fear not, little flock, for it is your Father's good pleasure to give you the kingdom." It may seem strange, but I have recollected ever since, and still recollect the train of thought presented. He first made a statement of the estimated population of the earth. He then took out the pagans, and then the Mohammedans, and then the Jews. This left him Christendom. Christendom was small in comparison with the whole. He then cut off a great many from Christendom, and came down to the visible Church. Of course a great many members of the Church were unsound, whilst the sound membership was small. The flock was a little flock. I suppose my mind was in a situation to receive vivid impressions then. I thought of nothing but preaching, and preachers, and connected subjects. Robert Donnell followed Mr. Bell with a sermon, having reference to the death of Rev. William McGee, one of the fathers who had recently been called away. It was a very solemn and interesting day.

I have no recollection of seeing Mr. Bell after that meeting, until the fall of 1822, at the first meeting of the Cumberland Synod which I ever attended. This meeting was also held at the Beech. Mr. Bell was there as the Superintendent of Charity Hall. On that occasion, I began to see a little of what I have seen my full share since. Charity Hall was an institution of the Church, and it was already in need of money. This was its condition during the eight or ten years of its existence which followed. The labors, and discouragements, and varied toils of the superintendent and missionary were very great. Yet he bore all heroically. He left a record behind which the Church ought to read. Year after year he urged the claims of Charity Hall and the benighted condition of the Indians before the Synod and the Church. A few of the old ministers and of the old men and women stood by him to the last. No man could have commanded more of their confidence, and the record shows that their confidence was never betrayed. It was a good work, and, as far as the limited means would allow, it was well done; and when history does full justice to the characters and labors of those who have devoted themselves to the elevation and evangelization of the savage tribes of this country, the name of Robert Bell will be found worthy of a place with those of John Eliot, and David Brainerd, and others who have made themselves benefactors of their race.

www.ingramcontent.com/pod-product-compliance
Lightning Source LLC
Chambersburg PA
CBHW022122040426
42450CB00006B/804